what about...
the human body?

what about... the human body?

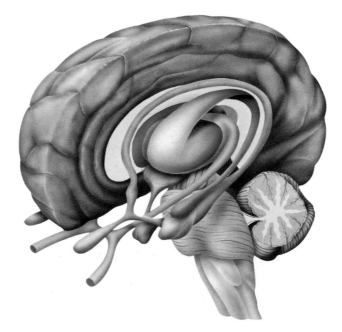

Steve Parker

PUBLISHING

First published in 2004 by Miles Kelly Publishing Ltd
Bardfield Centre, Great Bardfield, Essex, CM7 4SL

This edition printed in 2008 by Miles Kelly Publishing Ltd

4 6 8 10 9 7 5 3

British Library Cataloguing-in-Publication Data
A catalogue record for this book is available from the British Library

ISBN 978-1-84236-790-2

Printed in Thailand

Editorial Director Belinda Gallagher
Art Director Jo Brewer
Senior Editor Jenni Rainford
Assistant Editors Lucy Dowling, Teri Mort
Copy Editor Rosalind Beckman
Design Concept John Christopher
Volume Designers Jo Brewer, Michelle Cannatella
Picture Researcher Liberty Newton
Indexer Helen Snaith
Production Manager Elizabeth Brunwin
Reprographics Anthony Cambray, Liberty Newton, Ian Paulyn

www.mileskelly.net
info@mileskelly.net

www.factsforprojects.com

CONTENTS

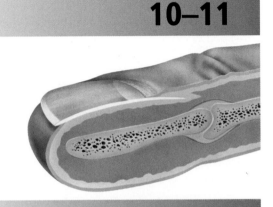
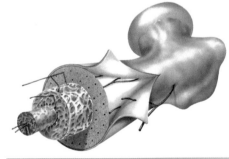
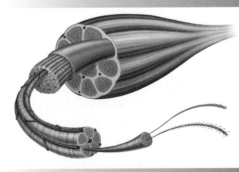
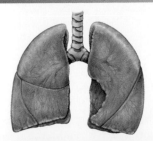
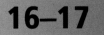

6 CONTENTS

Eating and Digestion

Why do we need to eat?
How many teeth do we have?
What happens before swallowing food?
What does the stomach do?
Which is the body's longest organ?
Which is the biggest internal organ?

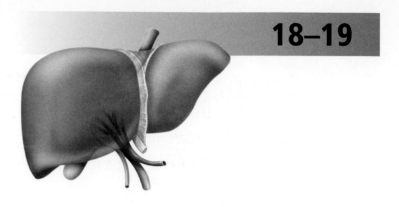

Heart and Blood

Which part of the body never rests?
How fast can the heart beat?
How much blood is in the body?
How many jobs does blood have?
What is a clot?

Body Wastes and Defences

What do the kidneys do?
How do wastes leave?
How much urine does the body make each day?
What do hormones do?
Is blood the only liquid flowing around the body?
What is the immune system?

Senses

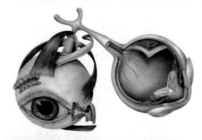

How do the eyes work?
What numbers 125 million in the eye?
Can we hear every sound?
What is inside the nose?
How does the tongue taste different flavours?

Nerves and Brain

Which body parts could stretch halfway to the Moon?
What is a motor nerve?
How many nerve cells are there?
How fast do nerves work?
How is the brain 'wired' into the body?

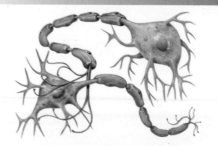

Working Brain

How does thinking happen?
Where are memories stored?
Are bigger brains more intelligent?
What is the mind's eye?
What happens during sleep?

Start of a New Body

How does the body begin?
Where do eggs come from?
Where do sperm come from?
How do egg and sperm join?
What are genes and inheritance?
Which kind of features are inherited?

The Body Before Birth

Which body parts develop first?
When does the heart start to beat?
Can an unborn baby hear?
How does the unborn baby breathe?
What happens at the start of birth?

The Growing Body

What does a newborn baby do?
When does walking start?
When does talking begin?
When does the body grow fastest?
When is the body fully-grown?

What do we know more about than anything else in the world? You! Perhaps not you as an individual, but the way you live, eat, drink, think, feel happy and sad, daydream and sleep – the human body. There are more than six billion human bodies in the world, and each and every one of those has unique characteristics but, inside, they are all made and work in much the same way.

How can we learn about the body?

Modern medical science uses hundreds of complex machines and tests to find out more about the body every year. They include scanners, chemical tests, microscopes and electrical monitors. Scanners and X-ray machines see inside the body. Chemical tests on the blood and other parts show the substances they contain. Microscopes reveal the smallest cells and even genes. Electrical devices, such as heart (ECG) and brain (EEG) monitors, show readings as wavy lines on a paper sheet or screen for doctors to examine.

❷ *A typical body cell is far too small to see without a microscope. Yet it contains many even smaller parts, called organelles.*

What are organs?

Body organs include the heart, brain, stomach and kidneys and are the body's main parts or structures. The biggest organ within the body is the liver, while the largest organ of the whole body is the skin. Usually, several organs work together as a body system.

Cell membrane (outer covering)

Nucleus (control centre)

Internal membranes (make cell products)

Mitochondria (energy centre)

❷ *Inside the arm are many organs and tissues, including bones, blood vessels and nerves. Muscles and connective tissues link all these parts together.*

What are body systems?

A body system is a group of parts that work together to carry out one job or particular task to help keep the body alive and working well. For example, the heart, blood vessels (tubes) and blood make up the circulatory system. This pumps or circulates blood all around the body, to supply every tiny part with essential substances such as oxygen and nutrients, and to collect wastes for removal.

Humerus (upper arm bone)

Radial artery and vein

Radius (forearm bone)

Carpals (wrist bone)

Discovering **the body**

Key **dates**

160 Galen of ancient Rome starts to carry out some of the first studies of the human body, seeing its insides through the terrible wounds suffered by gladiators.

1543 Andreas Vesalius produces the first detailed book of body anatomy, *On the Fabric of the Human Body.*

1610 The newly invented microscope reveals cells and other tiny body parts.

1628 William Harvey discovers that blood is pumped around the body by the heart, rather than continually being made and used up.

1895 Wilhelm Röntgen discovers X-rays and how they pass through flesh but not bone.

1900 Karl Landsteiner works out the system of blood groups, making blood transfusions safer.

1970s Early CT and MR scanners show detailed pictures of inside the body.

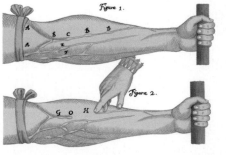

❶ *A diagram from William Harvey's book shows blood flow in veins in the arm.*

2000 The order of chemicals is worked out in the entire set of the body's genetic material, DNA, known as sequencing the human genome.

⊃ *Some body parts, such as bones and joints, can be replaced by artificial versions made of tough plastics, stainless steel and titanium. Artificial or prosthetic joints are shown here coloured in white.*

Can body parts be replaced?

Some body parts can be successfully replaced to enable the person to move about easily again. For example, people who have trouble with one or both of their hips, knees, shoulders, elbows or any of their fingers can be given metal or plastic artificial joints in place of the damaged body parts. Broken bones can be held together with plates, strips and screws. Some blood vessels can be replaced by manufactured plastic tubes. Internal organs, such as the heart, lungs, liver or kidneys, can be replaced. The new organs often come from deceased people who donated them before their death.

What are tissues?

Tissues are groups or collections of microscopic cells that are all the same type and do the same job. Examples include muscle tissue, which can shorten or contract to cause movement, nerve tissue, which carries nerve signals, and connective tissue, which fills the gaps between other tissues. Most organs are made of several kinds of tissue.

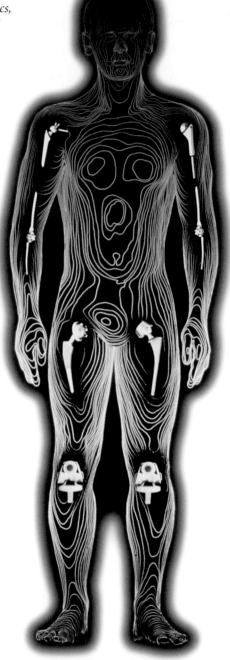

What are cells?

Cells are the smallest living parts of the body. They are like microscopic 'building blocks' in many shapes and sizes, which carry out different jobs. There are some 200 different kinds such as nerve cells, muscle cells and blood cells. On average, about 100 cells in a row would stretch across this 'o'. The whole body contains more than 50 billion billion cells.

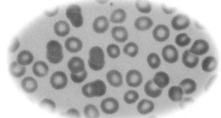

⬆ *Under a light microscope, magnified about 1,500 times, red blood cells appear as blobs with pale centres. This is due to their dished shape, rather like a doughnut.*

⬆ *Physiologists study how the body uses energy during strenuous activity such as swimming, when the heart beats faster, the lungs breathe more quickly and the muscles work harder.*

Body **imaging**

Ordinary X-rays – show the hardest, heaviest or densest body parts, such as bone, cartilage and teeth, as white or pale against a black background.
CT or CAT (computerized axial tomography) scans – use very weak X-rays to show bones and also softer parts such as blood vessels and nerves, in three dimensions.

MR or NMR (nuclear magnetic resonance) scans – use powerful magnetic fields and pulses of radio signals to show similar images to CT scans in even more detail.
Ultrasound scans – use the reflections or echoes of very high-pitched sound waves beamed into the body to build up an image such as an unborn baby in the womb.
Computers – all of these images can be given added colours by computers to make the details even clearer.

◐ *An X-ray defines the bones in the hand – and a ring worn on the finger.*

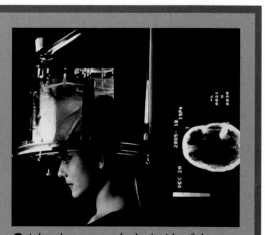

⬆ *A head scan reveals the inside of the brain as if 'sliced' into layers. Carrying out many scans at different levels builds up a 3-D structure of the brain and head.*

When you look at a human body, most of what you see is dead. The surface layer of the skin, and the hair and nails, were once made of living cells. But these gradually die off and then get rubbed or worn away as we move about, change clothes or wash and rub dry with towels, as part of daily living. The only visible parts of the body that are truly alive are the eyes.

Hair shaft
Epidermis
Touch sensor
Sebum gland
Hair follicle
Pressure sensor

⊙ The epidermis, the tough outer layer of skin, is mostly dead. The dermis below contains hair follicles, sweat glands, tiny blood vessels, and micro-fibres of elastin for flexibility, and collagen for toughness.

What is skin made of?

Like the rest of the body, skin is made of billions of microscopic cells. These cells form two layers, the epidermis on the outside and the dermis below it. The epidermis is tough and hard-wearing. The dermis is thicker and contains millions of microscopic sensors that detect different kinds of touch on the skin.

Why doesn't skin wear away?

It does – but it is always growing to replace the bits that wear away and are rubbed off. The tiny cells at the base of the epidermis continually multiply to make more cells. These gradually move upwards, filling with the tough substance keratin as they die, to form the hard-wearing surface. The whole skin surface is gradually worn away and replaced every four weeks.

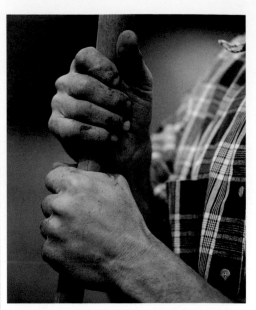

⊙ When undertaking hard physical work, the rubbing on the skin of the hands may be greater than normal. The epidermis (outer layer of skin) may develop calluses (rough patches of skin) against further damage.

How thin is skin?

Skin can be between 0.5 and 5 mm thick. The thinnest skin is found on the eyelids and other delicate, sensitive parts of the body. The thickest skin is on the soles of the feet. This can be 5 mm or more, and grows even thicker in people who often walk and run in bare feet. It grows thicker to adapt and protect the soles of the feet from damage.

⊙ An enlarged view of the skin shows surface flakes that are about to be rubbed off.

Skin, nail and **hair facts**

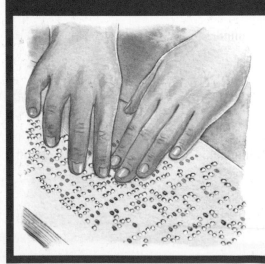

⊙ The sense of touch is vital to a person who is blind. Braille is a system of raised dots and patterns, which each symbolize different letters or words. Through the use of braille, a blind person can feel, and so read, the words on a page.

Skin **sensations**

Touch may seem like one sense. However, it is much more complex:

• There are at least seven different kinds of microsensors in skin. In sensitive areas such as the lips and fingertips, hundreds of microsensors are packed into an area the size of this 'o'.

• The sensors work together to detect light touch, heavy pressure, movements and vibrations, heat and cold – and the pain that warns us that skin may be damaged.

How quickly does hair grow?

In most people, if a single head hair was left uncut, it would grow about 1 m long, over four to five years. Then the hair naturally falls out of its follicle, which is the tiny pit in the dermis where it grows. However, this does not mean a bald head, since the follicle soon starts to grow a new hair. Follicles over the scalp do this at different times, so there are always plenty of hairs – in most people.

⊕ A hair is alive and growing only at its root, down in the base of the follicle. The shaft that sticks out of the skin is dead, and is made of flattened cells stuck firmly together.

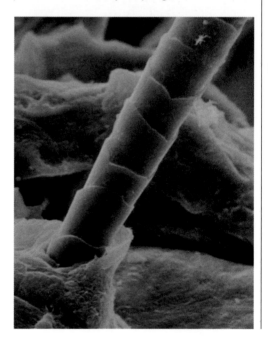

Why do we have fingernails?

To form a firm layer at the back of the fingertip. This stops the flexible fingertip from bending too much, so we can feel, press and pick up small items more easily and without damage. A nail grows at its root, which is under the skin at its base, and slides slowly along the finger.

⊕ Black hair is coloured by lots of melanin.

⊕ Reddish hair has carotenoid colouring substances.

➔ Light hair has less of the pigment melanin.

Lunula

Nail bed

Nail root

Finger bone

⊕ A nail has its root under the skin and grows along the nail bed, which is the skin underneath it. The paler, crescent-like area is the lunula or 'little moon'.

Why do people have different coloured hair?

Hair colour depends on the genes inherited from parents. The colour of both hair and skin is due to natural pigments, mainly the very dark brown substance melanin, contained in cells known as melanocytes at the base of the epidermis. In some people the melanocytes are more active and make more melanin, and so the skin and usually the hair are darker.

⊕ Eyelashes are among the thickest of hairs on the body, and are replaced quickly when they fall out.

Amazing **facts**

- A typical head hair grows up to 3.5 mm each week.

- An average person has between 100,000 and 120,000 head hairs on the scalp.

- There are many other hairs, including tiny ones over most of the body – up to 20 million in total!

- Each eyelash lasts only one to two months before it falls out, then a new one grows from the same follicle.

- A typical nail gets longer by about half a millimetre each week.

- The fingernails on the favoured hand grow slightly faster. So if you are left-handed, the nails on that hand grow faster than those on your right hand.

- All kinds of nails grow faster in the summer than the winter.

- Fingernails grow slightly faster than toenails.

Bones provide the strong framework that supports the whole body and holds its parts together. Without bones you would flop down on the floor like a jellyfish! All of the bones together are called the skeleton, and this gives protection as well as support.

Neck bones (cervical vertebrae)

Breastbone

Ribs

Hip bone (pelvis)

➔ *The skeleton has a total of 206 bones, including 32 in each arm, 31 in each leg, 29 in the head, 26 in the spinal column and hips, and 25 in the chest.*

Shin bone (tibia)

What do bones do?

Bones form a framework inside the body, which holds it upright, makes limbs such as the arms and legs strong and protects many internal organs. Long bones in the arms and legs work as rigid levers, so when muscles pull on them, they can push, lift or make other movements. Some bones are protective. The skull forms a hard case around the delicate brain, and the backbone, ribs and breastbone make a strong cage around the heart and lungs.

➔ *A typical bone has a hard outer layer, a spongy, honeycomb-like middle layer, and marrow at the centre, as well as tiny blood vessels and nerves.*

Periosteum (covering)

Hard bone layer

Spongy layer

Marrow

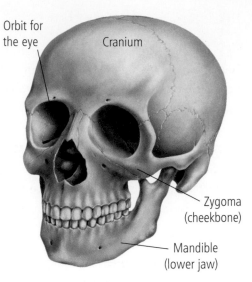

Orbit for the eye

Cranium

Zygoma (cheekbone)

Mandible (lower jaw)

➔ *The skull consists of 22 bones (including the lower jaw) linked by joints called sutures, which fix the bones firmly like glue. The sutures show up as faint wiggly lines.*

What is inside a bone?

A typical bone has three layers, which consist of collagen, minerals and bone marrow. On the outside is a 'shell' of compact or hard bone. This contains crystals of minerals such as calcium and phosphate for hardness, and fibres of collagen that allow the bone to bend slightly under stress. The middle layer is spongy or cancellous bone, with tiny spaces like a honeycomb. In the middle, the jelly-like bone marrow makes new cells for the blood.

Bone facts

Artificial joints

In some people, joints become stiff and painful due to disease, injury or stressful use over a long period of time. In many cases, these natural joints can be replaced with artificial ones – joint prostheses. These are usually made of supertough plastics and strong metals shaped like the original joint. An artificial hip allows some people to walk again without pain for 20 or more years.

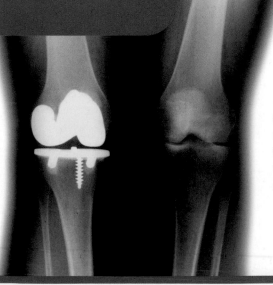

The spine (backbone)

The spine or spinal column is the body's central support. It is made of 26 block-like bones called vertebrae, one on top of the other, which hold up the skull and head while allowing the main body to flex and bend. The spinal column also protects the body's main nerve, the spinal cord, which links the brain to all body parts. The spinal cord is inside a tunnel formed by the lined-up gaps or holes within the vertebrae.

➔ *This artificial knee joint has two rounded plastic 'knuckles' at the base of the thigh bone, and a metal plate on top of the shin bone.*

What happens if a bone breaks?

It starts to mend itself straight away! Bones are made of living tissues, and once the parts of the bone are put back into their natural positions, usually by a doctor, microscopic cells called osteoblasts begin to make new bone that fills the break or gap. After a few months the gap is joined and the bone is repaired.

Are there different kinds of joints?

Yes, there are several different kinds, such as synovial joints, which allow movement, and suture joints, which do not. Synovial joints are found throughout the body, especially in the shoulder, elbow, hip and knee. These allow various kinds of movements, depending on their design. The elbow and knee are hinge joints, which allow only a to-and-fro movement. The shoulder and hip are ball-and-socket joints, which enable more flexibility such as twisting.

In the shoulder the ball-shaped end of the upper arm bone fits into a cup-like socket formed by the shoulder blade and collarbone.

Collarbone

Upper arm bone

What is inside a synovial joint?

In a synovial joint the ends of the bones have a covering of shiny, slippery cartilage. The joint also contains oil-like synovial fluid, which is made by a bag-like covering around the joint, the synovial capsule. This fluid moistens the cartilage, making movements smooth, with hardly any rubbing and wear. The bones are prevented from moving too far or coming apart by strap-like ligaments, which are strips of strong tissue holding the bones and joints together.

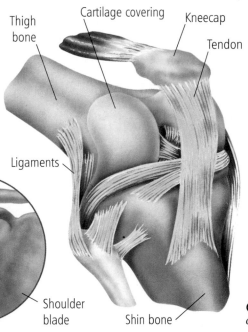

Thigh bone

Cartilage covering

Kneecap

Tendon

Ligaments

Shoulder blade

Shin bone

Regular exercise and movement help make joints flexible and supple to keep them healthy.

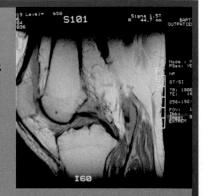

Do bones change with age?

Yes, a baby's bones are softer and more flexible than an adult's. They tend to bend, rather than snap, under stress, which is helpful because young children tend to fall over or suffer bumps quite often. A baby's skeleton also contains more than 340 bones compared to 206 in the adult skeleton. This is because in early life some bones merge with others to form one bone. All bones are fully formed and at their strongest between about 20 and 45 years of age. In later life the bones become stiffer and more brittle, so they tend to crack rather than bend.

Strap-shaped ligaments criss-cross the outside of the knee joint to hold the bones in place.

The spinal column has 26 bones called vertebrae. There are seven in the cervical or neck region, 12 in the chest (thorax), five in the lumbar or lower back region, and two at the base: the sacrum and the coccyx.

Cervical vertebrae

Thoracic vertebrae

Lumbar vertebrae

Sacrum

Coccyx

Amazing **bone facts**

- Most of the body parts are about two-thirds water, but bones are only one-fifth water.

- The skull has 22 bones, including 14 in the face and eight in the domed brain case or cranium.

- The smallest bones are the three tiny ossicles inside each ear.

- The longest bone is the thigh bone or femur, making up about one-quarter of the body's total height.

- The broadest bone is the hip bone or pelvis.

- Most people have 12 pairs of ribs, but about one person in 500 has 13 or 11 pairs.

A scan through the knee joint shows the oval-shaped patella or knee cap on the left, the joint itself in the centre and the rear leg muscles to the right.

Every movement, every breath, every mouthful you chew – all of these actions and more are carried out by the body's muscles. A single muscle can do only one task, which is to get shorter to pull on body parts. But working together in very precise and co-ordinated ways, the body's hundreds of muscles carry out thousands of different activities every day.

Occipitalis

Deltoid

◐ The muscles just under the skin are called the superficial layer. Beneath them are the intermediate or middle layer of muscles, and then the deep layer muscles, which are next to the bones.

Latissimus

Gluteus

Vastus

Gastrocnemius

How many muscles are there in the body?

There are about 640 muscles in the body. The biggest ones are in the torso, hips, shoulders and thighs. As you move you can see them bulging under the skin. But some muscles are much smaller. Each eyeball has six small ribbon-shaped muscles behind it, so it can swivel to look around.

◐ Inside a muscle are bundles of myofibres, each about as thick as a human hair. Every myofibre is made of even thinner myofibrils, which contain numerous strands of the substances actin and myosin. These slide past each other to make the muscle contract.

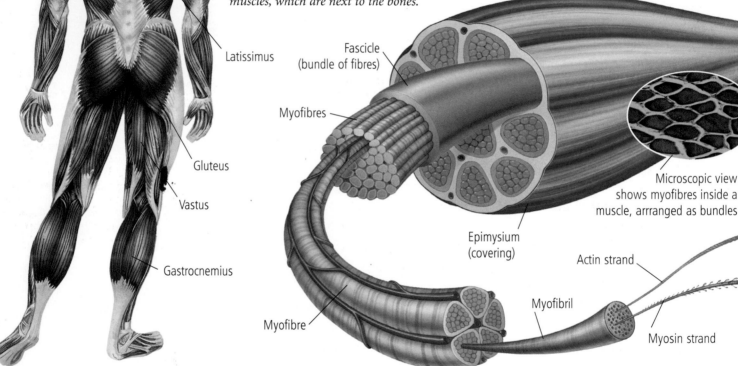

Fascicle (bundle of fibres)

Myofibres

Epimysium (covering)

Myofibre

Myofibril

Actin strand

Myosin strand

Microscopic view shows myofibres inside a muscle, arrranged as bundles

Reflexes – **look out!**

Reflex action
A reflex is a body movement that happens automatically, without any conscious control by the brain (without 'thinking'). Many reflexes help the body to avoid injury or damage, by making muscles contract to pull a part away from harm. For example, if an object comes fast towards the face, such as a ball in sport, the body has several reflexes for protection, all of which react within a fraction of a second:

- The eyelids close to guard the delicate surfaces of the eyes.
- The face 'screws up' as the facial muscles tense and harden.
- The neck and upper body muscles jerk the head out of the ball's path.
- The shoulder and arm muscles throw up the arms and hands to block the ball.

◑ When the finger feels pain, a reflex quickly pulls the hand away.

Brain

Nerve signals into spinal cord

Nerve signals to muscle

Finger detects pain

Nerve signals

Can muscles push?

No, they can only pull, or contract. Most muscles are long and slim, and connected at each end to bones. As the muscle contracts it pulls on the bones and moves them, and so moves that body part. Then another muscle on the other side of the bone contracts, to pull it back again. Muscles work like this in pairs or teams to move body parts to-and-fro.

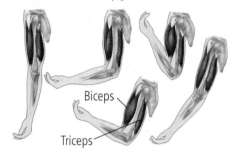

Biceps

Triceps

⬆ *Most muscles are arranged in opposing or antagonistic pairs to pull a bone one way and then the other, like the biceps and triceps in the upper arm.*

How fast can muscles work?

Very fast – as quick as the blink of an eye! But the speed depends on the type of muscle. 'Fast-twitch' muscles in the fingers, face and eyes can contract in less than one-twentieth of a second. They are speedy but soon tire. 'Slow-twitch' muscles, such as those in the back, take longer but can keep contracting for a greater period of time.

What controls muscles?

The brain controls muscles by sending nerve signals along nerves to the muscles, to tell them when to contract, by how much, and for how long. Luckily we learn many common movements such as walking, speaking and chewing early in life, so that we can do them almost without thinking. The brain is still in control, but it is the lower or 'automatic' part of the brain, which does not need our concentration or conscious awareness. Even standing requires muscle power, as the neck and back muscles tense to keep the body balanced and upright.

Why do muscles get tired?

Blood carries oxygen and energy to the muscles in order to keep them active, but the blood flow is sometimes too slow and so the muscles get tired. If the heart cannot pump blood fast enough to active muscles, the supplies run short and the muscles become tired or fatigued and can no longer work. Also, a busy muscle makes a waste product, lactic acid, which is taken away by blood. Again, if the blood supply is insufficient, lactic acid builds up in the muscle and may cause cramps.

Can the body make more muscles?

No, but the muscles it has can become larger, by undertaking exercise and activity. This helps the muscles stay healthier and the body become stronger, with added muscle power. Exercise also makes the heart pump faster and the lungs breathe harder, which has many benefits for the whole body. In fact the heart itself is mostly muscle, and the movements of breathing are muscle-powered, too. So any form of exercise helps to keep all muscles fit and healthy.

⬅ *As a tennis player serves, muscles are working not only in the arms, but in the neck, back and legs, to keep the body well-balanced and supple, in order to run forwards without causing injury.*

➡ *Exercise makes muscles larger and stronger. But practise, movement skills and muscle control techniques are also vital, especially in very physical actions, such as weighlifting. A good lifting technique helps to avoid strain and injury to the body.*

Amazing **facts**

- Muscles make up about two-fifths of the body's total weight.

- On average, men have a greater proportion of body weight as muscle, compared to women.

- The biggest muscle is the gluteus maximus in the buttock, used to push the leg back and body forwards when walking, running and jumping.

- The smallest muscle is the stapedius, deep in the ear, hardly thicker than this letter 'l'.

Stapedius muscle

Stirrup

⬆ *The tiny stapedius muscle pulls on the stirrup (stapes) bone inside the ear, during very loud noise to prevent damage to the ear's delicate inner parts.*

You might not think you are doing much at the moment – except reading, of course. But many parts of the body are busy. One of the vital processes that never stops is breathing, every few seconds during the day and all through the night, too. Along with the heartbeat, it is the body's most essential activity.

Nasal chamber

Throat

Voice-box (larynx)

Windpipe (trachea)

Left lung

Right lung

Diaphragm muscle

◆ The respiratory system includes the parts of the body specialized to take in oxygen from the air. Some parts have others uses too, such as smell in the nose, and speech in the voice-box (larynx).

Why do we need to breathe?

To get oxygen into the body. Oxygen is a gas which forms one-fifth of air. The body needs it for an inner chemical process that happens in every microscopic cell. It breaks down the high-energy substance glucose to release its energy for powering life processes. Oxygen is required for glucose breakdown. Since the body cannot store oxygen, it must always obtain new supplies.

Where does breathed-in air go?

Through the nose and down the throat, into the windpipe (trachea) in the neck, and then along air tubes called bronchi into the two lungs in the chest. All of these parts form the body's respiratory system. Breathing is sometimes called respiration or bodily respiration.

◆ Air flows to and from the lungs along the windpipe, which branches at its base into two bronchi, one to each lung. The heart fills the scoop-like space located between the lungs.

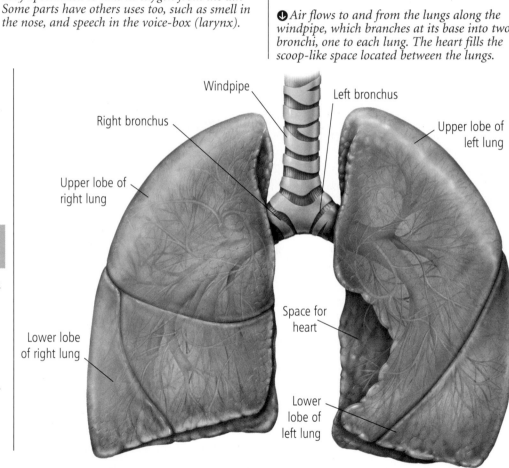

Windpipe

Right bronchus

Left bronchus

Upper lobe of left lung

Upper lobe of right lung

Space for heart

Lower lobe of right lung

Lower lobe of left lung

Breathing **facts**

Breathing muscles

Half a litre of air passes in and out of the lungs each time you breathe. Breathing uses the sheet-like diaphragm below the chest, and the strip-like intercostals between the ribs.

To breathe in, both muscle sets contract. The diaphragm changes from a domed shape, to a flatter shape, pulling down the bases of the lungs. The intercostal muscles force the ribs up and out pulling on the lungs. Both these actions stretch the spongy lungs to suck in air.

To breathe out, both muscle sets relax. The stretched lungs spring back to their smaller size, blowing out air.

➤ Breathing-in or inspiration (left) is powered by muscles and so uses energy. Breathing-out or expiration (right) is due to the stretched lungs becoming smaller, like an elastic band contracting, and so does not need muscle power.

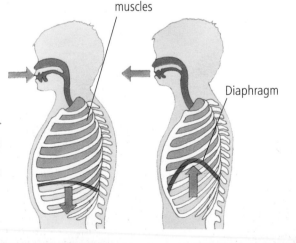

Intercostal muscles

Diaphragm

What are the lung's smallest parts?

Alveoli, which are shaped rather like miniature balloons. There are about 250 million alveoli in each lung! Each alveolus is wrapped in a network of even smaller blood vessels – capillaries. Oxygen from the air in the alveolus can seep easily into the blood in the capillaries, to be carried away around the body by the blood circulation.

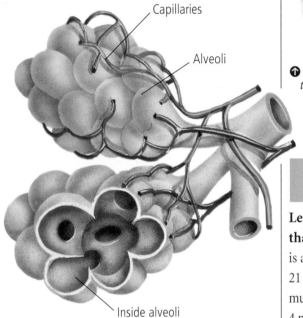

Capillaries

Alveoli

Inside alveoli

🔼 *The bubble-like alveoli are in groups or bunches at the ends of the narrowest air tubes, wrapped in blood capillaries. They make up about one-third of the total space taken up by the lungs.*

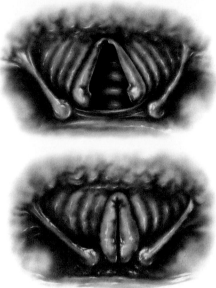

🔼 *The two vocal cords are in the voice-box in the neck. Each one sticks out from the side like a flexible flap. The cords have a triangular-shaped gap between them for normal breathing (top), and move almost together for speech (bottom).*

What is in breathed-out air?

Less oxygen but more carbon dioxide than is present in breathed-in air. There is about 16 per cent oxygen, compared to 21 per cent in breathed-in air. But there is much more carbon dioxide, more than 4 per cent compared to almost none in breathed-in air. Carbon dioxide is a waste product made by the breakdown of glucose for energy. If it builds up it will poison the body. So it is collected by the blood, passes into the air in the alveoli and is breathed out.

When is breathing out noisy?

When you talk, sing, hum, shout and scream. These sounds are made by the vocal cords inside the voice-box (larynx), at the top of the windpipe. As air passes up the windpipe, it blows through a narrow gap between the strip-like vocal cords and makes them vibrate to produce sounds. Breathing out harder makes the sounds louder, and stretching the cords longer makes the sounds higher-pitched.

🔽 *The basic sound of the voice comes from the vocal cords. But the shape and position of the air chambers in the throat, mouth, nose and sinuses (air-filled spaces in the skull bone) all affect the voice quality, so we all sound different.*

Yawning **facts**

- Yawning happens when the body has been still for a time, with shallow breathing, so more oxygen is needed. The body takes an extra-deep breath – the yawn.

- Yawning moves the jaw and face muscles and makes more blood flow to the brain, for greater alertness.

- Some people open their mouths to yawn so wide when they yawn forcefully that they dislocate or 'detach' their jaws and cannot close the mouth again.

Amazing **facts**

- As you rest or sleep, you breathe once every three or four seconds.

- After much exercise, you may breathe as fast as once each second.

- Deeper breathing moves 2–3 l of air each time.

- Restful breathing moves less than 10 l of air in and out of the lungs each minute, compared to more than 150 l during strenuous breathing.

- No matter how much you breathe out, about 0.5 l of air stays in your lungs.

- After holding your breath for a time, it is the amount of carbon dioxide in the body, dissolved in the blood, which causes gasping for air – not the lack of oxygen.

The body needs to breathe fresh air every few seconds to stay alive. But it cannot live on fresh air alone. Its other main needs are food and drink. The body needs food which contain many substances, used to help the body grow and repair itself, as well as provide the energy to move about. Drink is needed to continually replenish the supply of water in the bloodstream.

Why do we need to eat?

To provide energy for life processes, and to obtain many kinds of nutrients for bodily growth, maintenance and general health. Taking in food and breaking it into tiny pieces, small enough to absorb into the body, is known as digestion. Ten or so main parts, called the digestive system, work together to carry out this task. As swallowed food is moved through the digestive system, nutrients are absorbed into the bloodstream.

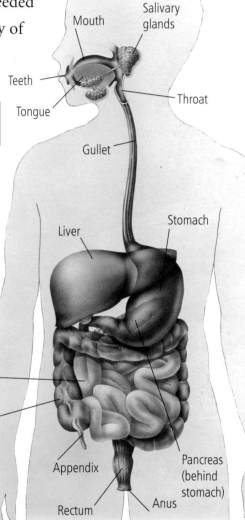

➡ *The digestive system includes the mouth, teeth, tongue, throat, gullet, stomach, the small and large intestines, which together form a long tube, the digestive tract, the liver and pancreas.*

Mouth
Salivary glands
Teeth
Tongue
Throat
Gullet
Liver
Stomach
Small intestine
Large intestine
Appendix
Rectum
Anus
Pancreas (behind stomach)

How many teeth do we have?

The human body has 52 teeth – but not all at once! The first set of 20 grow from around the time of birth to three or four years of age. They are called milk or deciduous teeth. From about six or seven years old, they fall out naturally as the second set of 32 teeth grow. These are larger and stronger, and are called the adult or permanent teeth.

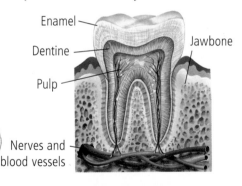

Incisors
Canine
Premolars
Molars

➡ *In each side of the jaw, the adult set of teeth includes two incisors at the front for biting, one taller canine for tearing, and two broad premolars, plus three wider molars for crushing and chewing.*

⬇ *In the centre of a tooth is a soft pulp of blood vessels and nerves. Around this is tough dentine. On the outside of the top part, the crown, is even harder enamel. The roots fix the tooth into the jawbone.*

Enamel
Dentine
Pulp
Jawbone
Nerves and blood vessels

The digestive system

⬅ *To help doctors investigate problems within the digestive system, patients drink barium meal, a special substance that shows up as white on an X-ray. This helps doctors to diagnose exactly what and where the problem might be.*

Timeline of digestion

0 hour – food is chewed and swallowed.
1 hour – food is churned with acids and juices in the stomach.
2 hours – partially-digested food begins to flow into the small intestine for further digestion and absorption.
4 hours – most food has left the stomach and passed to the small intestine.
6 hours – leftover and undigested foods pass into the large intestine, which takes the water and returns it to the body.
10 hours – the leftovers begin to collect in the last part of the system, the rectum, as faeces.
16–24 hours – the faeces pass through the last part of the system, the anus, and out of the body.

➔ *Swallowing involves a complicated series of muscle actions as the tongue pushes the lump of food (shown in yellow) into the throat, past the entrance to the windpipe and down the gullet.*

1 Tongue presses food to back of mouth

2 Food passes over the top of the windpipe

3 Food is pushed down the gullet

What happens before swallowing food?

The teeth bite off lumps of food, chew them and mix them with watery saliva (spit) to make the food soft and easy to swallow in small lumps. Food is swallowed into the gullet (oesophagus), a muscular tube that pushes it down through the neck into the stomach where it is churned around with gastric juices.

What does the stomach do?

The stomach breaks down food in two main ways. It is a muscular bag that can squeeze, mash and squash the food into a soft pulp. It also attacks the food by adding strong chemicals called acids and enzymes, which break down the food into a soup-like substance called chyme.

Which is the body's longest organ?

After the stomach, the semi-digested food flows into the body's longest part – the 6 m-long small intestine. This is coiled up in the middle of the lower body. It adds more enzymes and other chemicals to break the food into the smallest nutrients. These seep through the small intestine lining into the blood, and are carried away for use around the body.

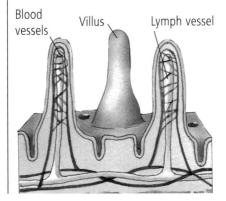

Blood vessels   Villus   Lymph vessel

Which is the biggest internal organ?

The liver, which is to the right of the stomach. It receives blood that is rich in nutrients, and processes or alters these nutrients so they can be stored or used around the body. To the left of the liver, under the stomach, is the pancreas. It makes powerful digestive juices that flow into the small intestine. The pancreas produces about 1.5 l of digestive juices each day.

↓ *The liver is a large, wedge-shaped organ with a plentiful blood supply, carried by the portal vein, direct from the intestines. It makes a fluid, bile, which is stored in the gall bladder and then flows into the small intestine, where the bile helps to digest fatty foods.*

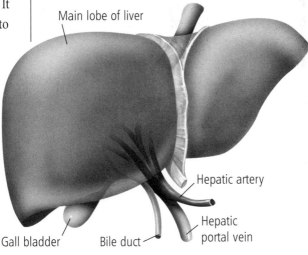

Main lobe of liver

Hepatic artery

Hepatic portal vein

Gall bladder   Bile duct

← *The inner lining of the small intestine is covered with small, finger-like parts, villi, each about 1 mm long. These provide a huge surface area for absorbing nutrients into the blood.*

Main **food groups**

↑ *Different kinds of food provide a varied selection of nutrients. The main food groups are shown in the panel on the right.*

The body needs a variety of substances in foods, called a balanced diet, to provide all the nutrients needed for good health:

Carbohydrates (sugars and starches) – used mainly for energy. They are found in bread, rice, potatoes, pasta, and various fruits and vegetables.

Proteins – vital for growth, to maintain and repair body parts, and for strong muscles and bones. They occur in most meats and fish, dairy products and some vegetables.

Oils and fats – provide some energy and building materials for body parts. Healthiest are plant-based oils. Too many fats from animal sources, especially fatty meats, are less healthy.

Vitamins and minerals – needed for many body processes, such as calcium for strong bones and teeth, and iron for blood. They are plentiful in fresh fruits and vegetables.

Fibre – not absorbed into the body, but keeps the digestive system working well. It is found in wholemeal bread, pasta and rice, fresh fruits and vegetables. Meat has little fibre.

The body is a busy place. Every second there are thousands of chemical processes inside every tiny cell, which use energy, nutrients and other raw materials, and produce unwanted wastes. The circulatory system is a complex network of blood vessels, such as arteries, veins and capillaries, specialized to bring these raw materials to every part of the body and take away the wastes – and it never stops.

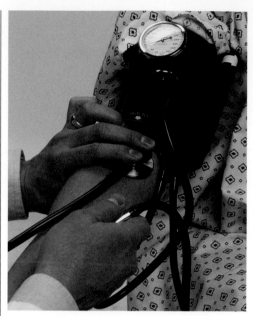

⬆ *Blood pressure can be measured by placing a cuff around the top of the arm and inflating it briefly. The reading then appears on a gauge that is connected to the cuff.*

Aorta (main artery) with branches to head and brain

Vena cava (main vein) from head and brain

To lungs

To lungs

From lungs

From lungs

Right atrium

Valve

Left ventricle

From lower body and legs

Right ventricle

To lower body and legs

⬅ *Inside the heart are four chambers. On each side are an upper atrium, which receives blood from the veins, and the lower thick-walled ventricle, which pumps it out into the arteries. One-way valves make sure blood flows in the correct direction.*

Which part of the body never rests?

The heart does not stop beating throughout life. It is a muscular bag that pumps blood round and round the body. The heart is divided into two pumps, left and right. The right pump sends used or stale blood to the lungs to pick up oxygen. The blood comes back to the left side, is pumped all around the body to deliver the oxygen, and then returns to the right side to complete the circulation. It takes blood an average of one minute to complete the whole journey.

How fast can the heart beat?

At rest the heart pumps about 60–75 times each minute, but after plenty of exercise this rises to 130 times or more, before returning to the resting rate. The speed of the heartbeat varies according to the body's needs. With each beat blood is pushed under pressure into the vessels and makes them bulge. This bulge can be felt in the wrist as the pulse. Doctors measure the pressure during and between heartbeats to tell how healthy the heart is.

In the blood

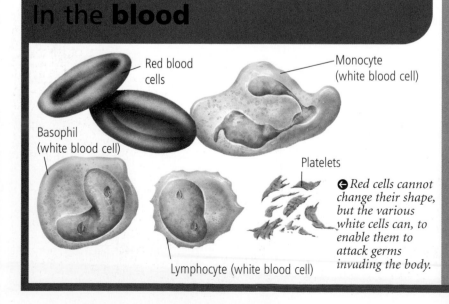

Red blood cells

Monocyte (white blood cell)

Basophil (white blood cell)

Platelets

⬅ *Red cells cannot change their shape, but the various white cells can, to enable them to attack germs invading the body.*

Lymphocyte (white blood cell)

Blood facts

In a drop of blood as big as this 'o' there are:

- About 20 million red blood cells, also called erythrocytes. Each one contains the substance haemoglobin, which easily joins to and carries oxygen. A typical red blood cell lives for about three months.

- Around 20,000 white blood cells, known as leucocytes. There are many kinds of white blood cells and most fight germs and illness (see page 23). Some live a few days, others for many years.

- Between one and two million platelets, or thrombocytes, for blood clotting.

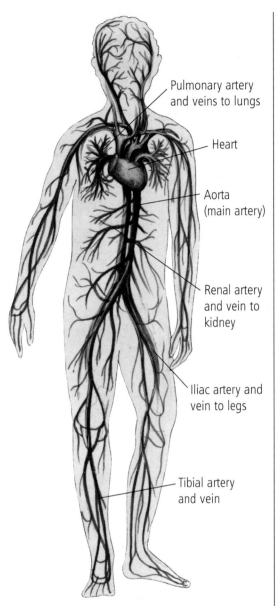

Pulmonary artery
and veins to lungs

Heart

Aorta
(main artery)

Renal artery
and vein to
kidney

Iliac artery and
vein to legs

Tibial artery
and vein

⬆ *The circulatory or cardiovascular ('cardio'
for heart, 'vascular' for blood vessels) system
includes a network of blood vessels which
transport blood to every part of the body.*

How much blood is in the body?

**About one-twelfth of the body's weight
is blood.** For most adults this means from
4–6 l. About 55 per cent of blood is a pale
liquid, plasma, containing dissolved oxygen,
nutrients and hundreds of other substances.
The remaining 45 per cent of blood
comprises microscopic cells.

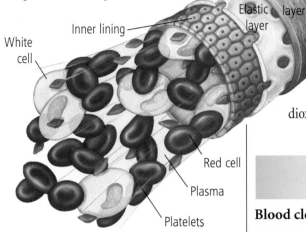

White
cell

Inner lining

Elastic
layer

Muscle
layer

Tough outer
cover

Red cell

Plasma

Platelets

⬆ *Red cells are the most numerous blood cells
and have a rounded, dished shape. White cells
can change their shape as they surround and
attack germs. Platelets are much smaller,
resembling pieces of cells.*

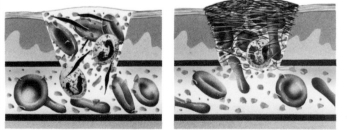

How many jobs does blood have?

Blood has more than 100 jobs to do.
One of the most important is to carry oxygen
in its billions of red blood cells. Blood also
distributes nutrients,
carries dozens of
natural substances
called hormones
that control body
processes, spreads
warmth around the
body, carries white cells that
fight disease, and collects carbon
dioxide and other wastes.

What is a clot?

**Blood clots or goes lumpy to seal a cut
or wound.** At the damage site, a substance in
blood, called fibrin, forms a tangled web of
micro-fibres. Blood cells, known as platelets,
help to form the clot, which stops blood
leaking away. The clot hardens into a scab,
which protects the area as
the damage heals over the
next few days, then falls off.

⬅ *Where there is a wound,
red and white cells tangle in
fibres (left). The lump hardens
to seal the gap (right).*

Types of **blood vessels**

There are five main types of blood vessels:
Arteries – carry blood away from the heart.
They have thick walls to withstand the surge
of high-pressure blood with each heartbeat.
They carry blood to the major parts or organs,
where they divide or branch into:
Arterioles – smaller versions of arteries, down
to the thickness of human hairs. These divide
more into:
Capillaries – the smallest blood vessels, less
than 1 mm long and far too thin to see.
Oxygen and nutrients seep from blood
through their walls into surrounding tissues.
Capillaries join to form:
Venules – which carry the slower-moving
blood, now under much less pressure, as they
join further into:
Veins – wide, thin-walled and floppy, which
take blood back to the heart.

At any moment about 66 per cent of all the
body's blood is in the veins, 29 per cent in
the arteries and 5 per cent in the capillaries.

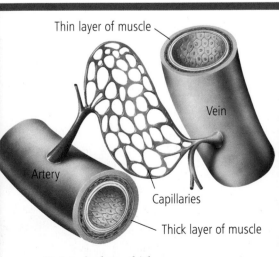

Thin layer of muscle

Vein

Artery

Capillaries

Thick layer of muscle

⬆ *Arteries have thicker,
stronger walls than veins.*

Wastes are produced by all living things, including the human body. Each day the body takes in 1–2 kg of foods, and 2–3 l of water. The unwanted parts and by-products from these 'inputs' must be removed daily, too. Otherwise after a year, the body would weigh more than one tonne and would be full of horrible, smelly wastes!

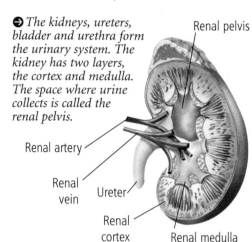

➔ *The kidneys, ureters, bladder and urethra form the urinary system. The kidney has two layers, the cortex and medulla. The space where urine collects is called the renal pelvis.*

Renal pelvis

Renal artery

Renal vein

Ureter

Renal cortex

Renal medulla

What do the kidneys do?

The two kidneys make the waste liquid, urine. Inside each kidney are one million microscopic filters called nephrons. Each has a tiny bunch of blood capillaries, which pass water and many substances into a long, looped tube. In the tube some of the water and substances are taken back into the body, leaving the unwanted water and wastes as urine. This flows from the kidney down a tube, the ureter, to the bladder.

How do wastes leave?

The body removes its wastes in three main ways – respiration, defecation and urination. Respiration (breathing), gets rid of carbon dioxide. Defecation, or bowel movements, removes the undigested and leftover parts of food and drink from the intestines. Urination gets rid of amounts of urine, a liquid containing urea and other unwanted substances filtered from the blood.

How much urine does the body make each day?

On average, the body makes about 1,500 ml of urine every 24 hours. The urine collects in the bladder until there is about 300 ml, when you feel the need to empty the bladder. This happens by urination along a tube to the outside, the urethra. However, the amount of urine varies hugely, depending on how much you drink, and if water is lost as sweat rather than as urine.

What do hormones do?

Hormones are natural body chemicals that control many internal processes and make sure the organs and systems work together. Hormones are made in parts called endocrine glands and travel around the whole body in the blood, but each hormone affects only certain parts, known as its target organs.

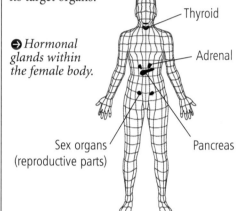

➔ *Hormonal glands within the female body.*

Thyroid

Adrenal

Sex organs (reproductive parts)

Pancreas

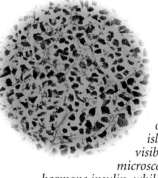

➔ *In the pancreas, this collection of millions of tiny clumps of cells called islets, only visible under a microscope, make the hormone insulin, while the cells around them make digestive juices.*

Body chemistry

Renal dialysis

In some cases the kidneys do not work properly and wastes build up in the blood. Many such people can be treated by renal dialysis using an 'artificial kidney'. The blood is led along a tube from the body to the dialysis machine, which filters out the waste products and returns it to the body. This usually takes a few hours, several times each week. Other treatments include passing fluid through the abdomen to soak up wastes and then removing it, or a kidney transplant.

➔ *During dialysis the patient must stay still and rest, as blood is led to the machine and back into the body along tubes, which are connected to the body.*

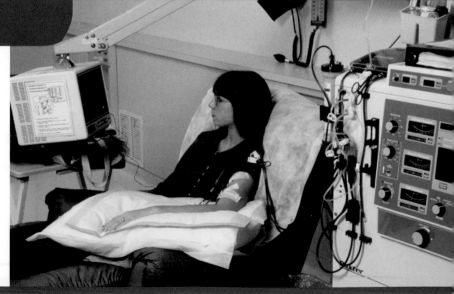

⬇ *Lymph nodes vary from less than 1 mm to about 20 mm across. They contain lymph fluid, which flows slowly around the body through lymph vessels. The nodes enlarge or swell greatly during illness as they fill with disease-fighting white cells.*

Capsule (outer layer)

Outgoing lymph vessels

White blood cells

Incoming lymph vessels

Adenoids

Tonsils

Thyroid gland

Armpit lymph nodes

Spleen

Main lymph vessel

Groin lymph nodes

Is blood the only liquid flowing around the body?

No, lymph fluid also flows through the body. Lymph fluid carries wastes of metabolism, and white blood cells, which destroy harmful substances such as germs. However, unlike blood, the fluid only moves one way. It begins as liquid around and between cells and tissues. It collects in small tubes called minor lymph vessels. These join to form major lymph vessels. The largest lymph vessels empty the lymph fluid into the main blood vessels near the heart. The body contains about 1–2 l of lymph fluid.

What is the immune system?

The body's self-defences, which attack invading germs and prevent illness, are called its immune system. Many white cells take part in fighting disease. Macrophages are large white cells that 'eat' germs whole. Lymphocytes make substances known as antibodies that stick to germs and disable them. Basophils are involved in allergic reactions and blood clotting. White cells are especially numerous in small areas called lymph nodes, which are sometimes called 'lymph glands'.

⬆ *The immune system includes many lymph nodes, found particularly in the neck, chest, armpits, lower body and groin. There are also lymph tissues in the adenoids, tonsils and the spleen, which sits behind the stomach.*

Hormones **and more hormones**

➡ *The pituitary gland is under the front part of the brain.*

Pituitary gland

⬅ *The thyroid gland is in the front of the neck.*

Pea-sized pituitary gland – just under the brain makes about ten hormones that control other endocrine glands, body growth and the reproductive (sex) organs.

Thyroid gland – in the neck makes hormones that control the cells' use of energy and the level of calcium in the blood.

Adrenal gland – on top of each kidney produces hormones (adrenaline) for coping with stress, which prepares the body for action, and hormones to regulate the kidneys and water balance.

Pancreas – in addition to making digestive juices, also produces the hormones insulin and glucagon, which control how quickly cells break down sugar for energy.

Reproductive organs – make hormones, mainly oestrogen and progesterone in ovaries in women, and testosterone in testes in men.

Other hormone-making organs – stomach, intestines, heart and kidneys also make some hormones.

Are you a sensitive person? Of course – your body has senses! The five main ones are sight, hearing, smell, taste and touch. They provide information about what is happening around and on the body, and in the nose and mouth. There are also tiny sensors inside the body that give information about the positions of the muscles and joints.

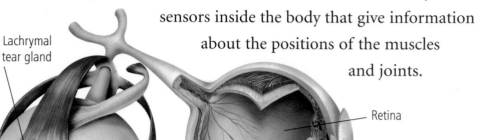

Lachrymal tear gland

Retina

Lens

Sclera

Lachrymal duct

Pupil

Iris

⬅ *Tear fluid is made in the lachrymal glands and drains from the inner eyelids through the lachrymal ducts into the nose. Inside the eye is the light-sensitive lining, the retina.*

Outer ear flap

Cartilage in ear flap

Ear canal

Skull bone

⬆ *The vibrations of sound waves pass along the ear canal to the eardrum, and along the tiny ear bones (ossicles) to the coiled cochlea, which converts them to nerve signals.*

How do the eyes work?

The eye changes the brightness and colours of the light rays it sees, into a code of electrical nerve signals, which it sends to the brain. The light rays pass through the domed, clear front of the eye, the cornea, then through a hole, the pupil, in a ring of coloured muscle,

⬇ *The eye's own lens, just behind the dark hole or pupil, can become thicker or thinner to focus on near or far objects. When the lens is not working properly, some people need extra lenses, so spectacles or contact lenses help them see clearly.*

the iris. The iris makes the pupil smaller in bright conditions, preventing too much light from entering the eye and damaging the inside.

What numbers 125 million in the eye?

Microscopic light-detecting cells called rods and cones, which make nerve signals when light rays shine on them. The 120 million rods see well in dim light but not colours. Up to six million cones work only in brighter light, but see colours and fine details. All these cells are in a curved sheet, which is as big as your thumb-tip and thinner than this page, called the retina. The retina lines the inside of the eyeball.

Making sense

Colour vision

There are three kinds of cone cells. Red cones are not red, they are so named because they respond only to red light. Blue cones detect blue light and, likewise, green cones make nerve signals only when green light shines or them. All the thousands of different colours, shades and hues we can see are worked out by the brain from combinations of signals from these three types of cones. Occasionally, one type of cone is missing, which causes a problem with identifying some colours.

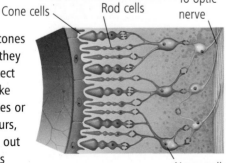

Cone cells

Rod cells

To optic nerve

Nerve cells

⬆ *Rod and cone cells in the retina pass their signals along nerve cells to the optic nerve.*

Amazing sense facts

• The taste buds of the tongue detect only four main flavours – sweet, salty, sour and bitter. The many tastes of different foods come from different strengths and combinations of these four.

• In contrast, the nose can detect more than 10,000 different smells and odours.

• As we eat, the tongue tastes – but the nose also smells the many different odours floating around the back of the mouth and up into the nasal chamber.

• What we think of as the 'taste' of a meal is not just flavours but also the sensation of many odours.

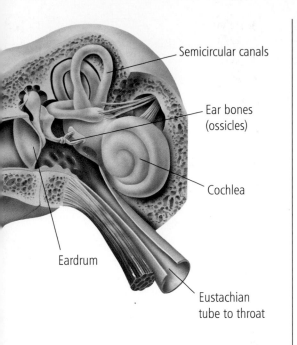

Semicircular canals

Ear bones (ossicles)

Cochlea

Eardrum

Eustachian tube to throat

What is inside the nose?

An air space called the nasal chamber, as big as your two thumbs. In its roof are two patches, each about as large as a thumbnail, called olfactory epithelia. Each of these has more than 25 million microscopic olfactory receptor cells. Tiny smell-carrying particles called odorants float through on breathed-in air and land on the cells, causing them to send nerve signals to the brain. However, each of the millions of cells responds to only a few kinds of odorants.

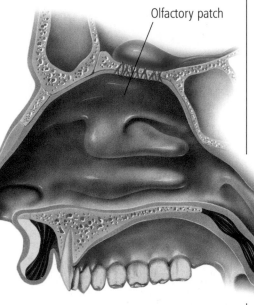

Olfactory patch

The hairy-looking patches called olfactory epithelia, which detect smells, are in the top of the air space known as the nasal chamber, inside the nose and above the mouth.

Can we hear every sound?

No, some sounds are too high-pitched (ultrasonic) or too low (infrasonic) for our ears – but some animals such as dogs and horses can hear them.
Sound waves in air travel along the tube-like ear canal and hit the eardrum, making it vibrate. The vibrations pass along three tiny bones, the ossicles, into the fluid inside the snail-shaped cochlea, deep in the ear. The vibrations shake micro-hairs sticking up from delicate hair cells in the cochlea, and these produce nerve signals, which are sent to the brain.

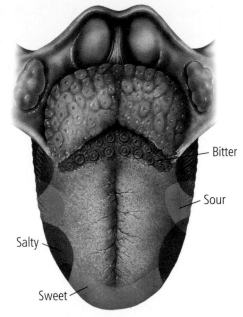

Bitter

Sour

Salty

Sweet

The taste buds at the tip of the tongue sense mainly sweet flavours. Those at the sides detect salty and, behind them, sour, with bitter tastes sensed mainly across the tongue's rear.

How does the tongue taste different flavours?

As we eat, about 10,000 taste buds scattered around the tip, sides and rear of the tongue detect tiny particles in foods called flavourants. Each taste bud has around 25 gustatory receptor cells. If a suitable flavourant lands on a cell, it sends nerve messages to the brain. The tongue tastes flavours similarly to how the nose smells odours.

Jet take-off
120–140 dB

Motorcycle
70–90 dB

Vacuum cleaner
60–80 dB

Talking
40–60 dB

Whispering
20–30 dB

The loudness or intensity of sounds is measured in decibels, dB. Sound volumes of more than about 90 dB can damage the ears, especially if they are high-pitched and continue for a long time.

Sniffing helps the smell particles to swirl up into the roof of the nasal chamber within the nose, where the odour-detecting cells are situated.

Direction of sounds
We know the direction of sounds, such as from the left or right, because we have two ears. This is known as stereophonic or binaural hearing.

• Sound waves travel through air at about 340 m/sec. A sound from the left reaches the left ear first, and the right ear less than one-thousandth of a second later.
• The ear facing the sound's direction hears sounds more loudly than the other ear because sounds fade as they travel.
• The brain works out these time and volume differences to tell the sound's direction.

The body has its very own 'Internet'. This sends millions of signals along thousands of routeways called nerves, to-and-fro between its hundreds of parts, and to and from the one part which controls all the others – the brain. The brain is linked to the body by the main nerve, the spinal cord.

Which body parts could stretch halfway to the Moon?

The body's complicated network of branching nerves. If all the nerves could be joined together end to end, including the tiniest ones visible only under a microscope, they would stretch this far! Nerves are like shiny, pale cords. They are made of bundles of even thinner parts, nerve cells or neurons, which pass messages between each other. Each nerve has a tough covering to prevent squashing or kinking.

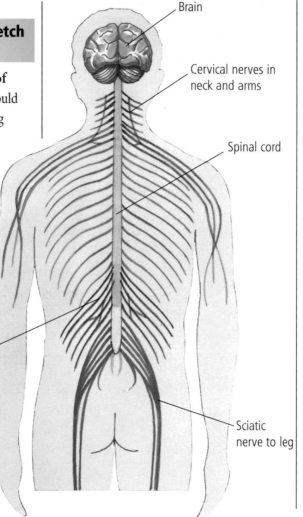

Brain

Cervical nerves in neck and arms

Spinal cord

Abdominal nerves

Sciatic nerve to leg

➡ *The nervous system controls and co-ordinates all body processes and activities. Its main parts are the brain and main nerve, the spinal cord, which together are called the central nervous system, and the hundreds of nerves that branch from them all through the body, the peripheral nervous system.*

What is a motor nerve?

A motor nerve carries nerve signals from the brain, out to the rest of the body. Nerve signals or impulses are tiny bursts of electricity that travel along nerves, carrying information. Most of these go to the muscles, telling them when to contract, by how much and for how long. Some motor signals go to glands, such as the sweat, salivary and tear glands, instructing them to release their contents. Sensory nerves carry signals the other way, from the eyes, ears and other sense organs, to the brain.

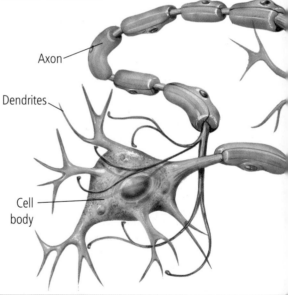

⬇ *A single nerve cell or neuron has a wide part, the cell body, with branching parts known as dendrites, which receive signals from other nerve cells. One long fibre-like part, the axon, passes the signals to other nerve cells.*

Axon

Dendrites

Cell body

How nerve **cells 'talk'**

Synapses

Nerve cells pass signals between each other at specialized links or junctions called synapses. However, the nerve cells do not actually touch at a synapse. They are separated by a very narrow gap, the synaptic cleft, which is 0.000025 mm (25 nanometres) across – less than one-hundredth the width of a hair. The signal passes across the fluid-filled gap as particles of chemicals known as neurotransmitters. However, this happens very fast, in less than one-thousandth of a second for each signal.

➡ *At a synapse, the axon end of one nerve cell almost touches the dendrite of another nerve cell. The nerve signal passes along the axon in electrical form but 'jumps the gap' as chemical particles, neurotransmitters, that slot into receptor sites on the receiving cell.*

Axon

Sending nerve cell

Neurotransmitters ready to be released

Synaptic cleft

Neurotransmitters cross the gap

Receiving nerve cell dendrite

Receptor site

⬆ *Under the microscope, a nerve cell growing in a glass dish sends out tentacle-like dendrites to 'search' for other nerve cells.*

How many nerve cells are there?

Hundreds of billions, including about 100 billion in the brain itself. The optic nerve from each eye to the brain has more than one million nerve fibres, and other nerves also have huge numbers. Also some nerve cells pass messages to more than 10,000 others, at synapses. So the possible number of pathways for nerve signals around the body is too big to imagine – and the connections continuously change, too.

➡ *As a person plays the guitar, the brain sends thousands of nerve signals every second along motor nerves to the muscles in the arms, hands and fingers, controlling movement with amazing speed and precision.*

How fast do nerves work?

The fastest signals, such as those from the skin, warning of damage and pain, go at more than 100 m/sec. This enables quick reflex action to protect the body from harm. However, the speed varies with the type of nerve it is and the information it carries. Other signals, such as those controlling how the stomach and guts work, can travel as slow as 1 m/sec.

Spinal cord

Vertebra (backbone)

Nerve roots

Spinal nerves

⬆ *The spinal cord is protected inside a tunnel, which is formed by a row of holes through the vertebrae (backbones).*

How is the brain 'wired' into the body?

By the spinal cord. This is the body's main nerve, and extends from the base of the brain down inside the backbone (spinal column). Thirty-one pairs of nerves branch from it, on each side, out into the body. There are also 12 pairs of nerves that branch from the brain itself, mainly to parts such as the eyes and ears. These are called cranial nerves and some extend down to the chest.

Amazing **brain facts**

- Ordinary or 'plain' X-rays do not show up softer parts very well, so they cannot reveal the details of the brain.

- A substance that shows up on X-ray, called a radio-opaque dye, can be injected into the bloodstream to show the blood vessels in and around the brain. This can reveal a blockage, as happens in a stroke.

- CT and MR scans (see page 9) show the brain in great detail, revealing the hollow fluid-filled chambers inside, called ventricles.

- PET (positron emission tomography) scans show how fast the various parts of the brain use energy, and so which parts are 'thinking' most.

⬆ *A doctor studies brain or whole-body scans to check for illness, harmful growths or injury inside the body.*

The brain never truly 'sleeps'. Even while most of the body is relaxed and still at night, the brain is busy. It controls the beating of the heart, the breathing lungs, body temperature, the digestive system and many other internal processes. The more we find out about the brain and its processes, the more complicated it seems.

How does thinking happen?

Thinking seems to happen as a result of nerve signals passing between many different parts of the brain. There is no single part in the brain where thoughts occur. Especially important is the cortex, which is the wrinkled grey outer layer of the large, bulging parts known as cerebral hemispheres. Under these are the lower parts of the brain, which are concerned less with consciousness or awareness, and more with 'automatic' processes such as controlling heartbeat and breathing. The smaller, lower, wrinkled part at the rear of the brain is the cerebellum. It organizes nerve signals sent to muscles, to ensure that all the body's movements are smooth and co-ordinated.

Cortex of cerebral hemisphere

Sulcus (groove)

Cerebellum

Brain stem

Pons

Hippocampus

Thalamus

Hyphothalamus

Corpus callosum (links two hemispheres)

Where are memories stored?

As with thinking, there is no single 'memory centre' in the brain but many parts working together to store memories, as pathways for nerve signals through the incredible maze of nerve cells. However, a curved part called the hippocampus is important in changing short-term memories, such as a phone number we need for just a few seconds, into long-term memories that we can recall weeks or months later.

⬆ *About nine-tenths of the brain is the large dome of the two cerebral hemispheres. The outer cerebral cortex is where many conscious thoughts happen. Inside are blob-like parts called ganglia.*

Brain **facts**

⬅ *The spikes and dips of an EEG recording show the brain's level of activity at different times, revealing health problems such as a stroke or epilepsy.*

Amazing **facts**

- An average brain weighs about 1.4 kg and occupies the top half of the head.

- Men have slightly larger brains than women, because the average man is bigger than the average woman.

- Compared to body size however, women have slightly larger brains than men.

- The brain is surrounded by three sheet-like membranes, the meninges, under the skull bone. These contain a watery liquid called cerebro-spinal fluid. The brain floats in this fluid, which cushions it from knocks and jolts.

Are bigger brains more intelligent?

No, there is no link between brain size and intelligence. It also depends what we mean by 'intelligence'. Some people are not especially successful at mathematics or science, but they may be brilliant at music or painting, or making money, or developing friendships. Every person has different abilities, talents and ways of behaving.

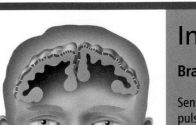

⬆ *Doctors examine brain scans to locate problems such as a stroke, when the blood supply to part of the brain fails and its nerve cells are damaged.*

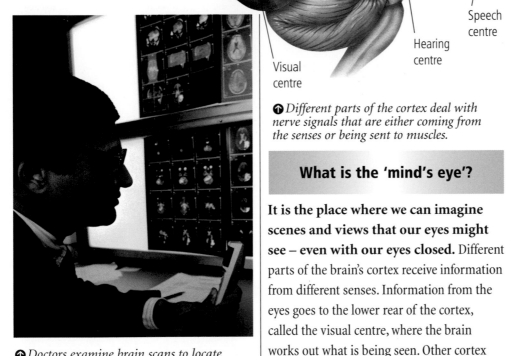

Touch centre   Movement centre

Speech centre

Hearing centre

Visual centre

⬆ *Different parts of the cortex deal with nerve signals that are either coming from the senses or being sent to muscles.*

What is the 'mind's eye'?

It is the place where we can imagine scenes and views that our eyes might see – even with our eyes closed. Different parts of the brain's cortex receive information from different senses. Information from the eyes goes to the lower rear of the cortex, called the visual centre, where the brain works out what is being seen. Other cortex centres are shown above. The movement centre is also called the motor cortex.

What happens during sleep?

EEG (electroencephalogram) recordings of the brain's nerve signals or 'brain-waves' suggest that, during sleep, the brain could be assessing recent events and memories, and deciding which ones are less important and can be forgotten. At certain times the body's muscles twitch and the eyes flick to-and-fro even though they are closed. This is called rapid eye movement or REM sleep and is when dreams occur.

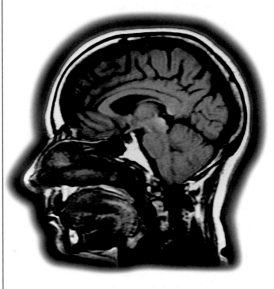

⬆ *This MR head scan shows how the wrinkled cerebral hemisphere dominates the brain. The lower rear of the brain tapers into the brain stem and then into the spinal cord in the neck.*

Inside the **head**

⬆ *Much of the brain is above eye level.*

Brainwaves

Sensor pads on the head pick up the very faint electrical pulses of nerve signals that are always passing around the brain, and display them on a screen or paper sheet.

These wavy lines are called EEGs (electroencephalograms).

The shapes of the waves change depending on whether the brain is fully alert and thinking hard, daydreaming, drowsy or fast asleep.

Even during sleep the waves change shape, especially between deep sleep, and lighter REM or 'dream' sleep.

The cortex and lobes

The brain's main outer surface, the cerebral cortex, contains billions of nerve cells linked together by trillions of connections.

If the wrinkled, grooved cortex was spread out flat, it would cover the area of a pillow-case, and be almost as thin – it is just a few millimetres in thickness.

The folds of the cortex reveal the main pairs of bulges or lobes of the brain. These are the frontal lobes under the forehead, the parietal lobes on the top of the head, the temporal lobes at the sides under the temples and the occipital lobes at the rear.

About four weeks after a new baby is born, we say it is 'one month old'. But really it has been ten months since its body began to form. After fertilization, the unborn baby spent nine months developing and growing inside its mother. People look carefully at babies to see who they resemble most, the mother or the father. This resemblance is due to the inheritance of genes.

How does the body begin?

In the beginning, every human body begins as a single cell. This is a tiny speck, smaller than the dot on this 'i', called the fertilized egg. It is made from the joining of two cells, the egg cell from the mother and the sperm cell from the father. As the human body develops over the following months and years, it is built up from billions and billions of microscopic cells, which are all formed by the splitting or division of other cells.

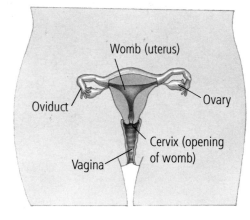

Womb (uterus)

Oviduct

Ovary

Cervix (opening of womb)

Vagina

Where do eggs come from?

Egg cells are contained inside a woman's body in rounded parts called ovaries, one in either side of the lower abdomen. Each ovary contains many thousands of egg cells. Each month one of these eggs develops and becomes ripe or ready to be fertilized. The ripe egg is released into a tube, the oviduct (fallopian tube), and passes slowly towards the womb, in a process called ovulation. The lining of the womb is thick and rich with blood, ready to nourish the egg if it is fertilized by a sperm cell. If not, the egg and the womb lining are lost through the birth canal or vagina, as the monthly menstrual flow or period.

The parts of the body specialized to produce a baby are known as the reproductive organs. In the woman, egg cells are contained in the two ovaries. Each month the menstrual cycle causes one egg to ripen and pass along the oviduct into the womb, where a sperm cell may join with it.

Where do sperm come from?

Sperm cells develop and are contained inside a man's body. They are made continually in rounded parts called testes, which hang below the lower abdomen inside a bag of skin called the scrotum. Millions of sperm cells are made each day. The sperm develop and are stored in a coiled tube called the epididymis. The sperm live for about one month. If they are not released from the body during sex, they gradually die and break apart as new ones are made.

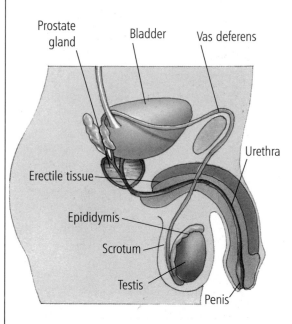

Prostate gland

Bladder

Vas deferens

Urethra

Erectile tissue

Epididymis

Scrotum

Testis

Penis

In a man's reproductive organs, sperm are made in the two testes. During sex they pass along the vas deferens tubes, which join and continue as the urethra, to the outside.

Genes and DNA

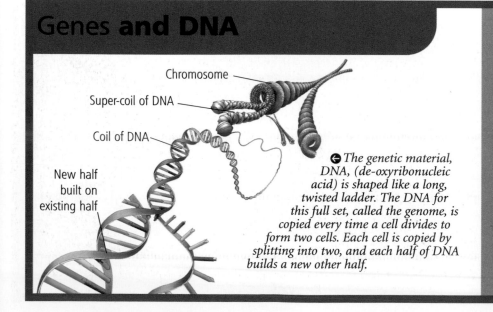

Chromosome

Super-coil of DNA

Coil of DNA

New half built on existing half

The genetic material, DNA, (de-oxyribonucleic acid) is shaped like a long, twisted ladder. The DNA for this full set, called the genome, is copied every time a cell divides to form two cells. Each cell is copied by splitting into two, and each half of DNA builds a new other half.

Amazing facts

- The full set of genetic material for a human body to develop contains about 30,000 genes.

- The full set of DNA is found in every cell in the body, located in the cell's control centre, or nucleus.

- The full set of DNA is in the form of 46 separate lengths, and each length is coiled or wound up very tightly to form an X-shaped part, the chromosome.

- If all the DNA from all the 46 chromosomes in a single cell were joined together, it would stretch almost 2 m.

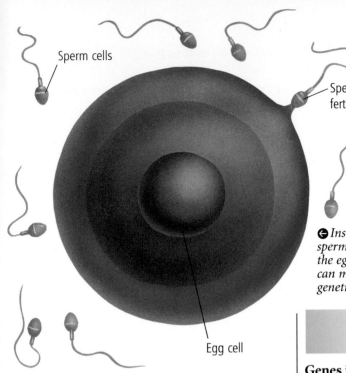

Sperm cells

Egg cell

Sperm cell
fertilizing egg cell

Sperm tail

Nucleus

Cap

⬆ *A single sperm cell has a rounded head containing genetic material (DNA).*

⬅ *Inside the oviduct of the woman, many sperm cells lash their tails to swim towards the egg cell. However, only one sperm cell can merge with the egg cell, adding its genetic material (DNA) to the egg's.*

How do egg and sperm join?

During sex (sexual intercourse), sperm cells enter the woman's vagina, swim through the womb and into the two oviducts where a ripe egg may be present. The journey begins inside the man's body where millions of sperm cells pass from the testes and epididymis, along tubes known as the vas deferens, to another tube called the urethra, which is inside the penis. Fluid containing the sperm leaves the end of the penis, but only one sperm can join with the egg at fertilization to start the new baby.

What are genes and inheritance?

Genes instruct the human body how to develop and carry out its life processes, and inheritance is the passing of these genes from parents to offspring. Genes are in the form of a chemical substance called DNA (de-oxyribonucleic acid). The egg cell contains genes from the mother, and the sperm cell contains the father's genes. When egg and sperm join at the time of fertilization, the genes come together and the fertilized egg can begin to develop into a baby.

Which kind of features are inherited?

Some physical body features are inherited from parents, such as the colour of the eyes, skin and hair, the shapes of the nose and ears, and overall body height. But some of these features can be controlled by several genes. This means a child's hair colour or ear shape is not always the same as either of the parents – it may be more similar to one of the grandparents. Even identical twins, with the same genes, have slightly different features.

⬇ *The full set of genes is contained in 23 pairs of chromosomes (below left). In reproduction the pairs split so that only 23 go into each egg or sperm (below centre). At fertilization, sets of 23 come together to form 46 (below right). The last pair of chromosomes determine the sex of the baby. The combination shown here is XY, with the large X and smaller x-like Y, and results in a boy. Two larger sex chromosomes, XX, would produce a girl.*

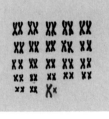

IVF and assisted reproduction

Sometimes a woman and man wish to have a baby, but are unable to. There are many causes, such as previous illness, so that the reproductive parts do not work properly. In some cases medical techniques known as IVF, in vitro fertilization, can help. In one method, egg cells are removed from the woman's ovaries through a narrow telescope-like tube, a laparoscope, inserted through a small incision (cut) in the skin. The egg cells are added to sperm cells in a shallow dish and observed under the microscope. If an egg and sperm join and the fertilized egg begins to grow, it is put into the woman's womb to continue its development.

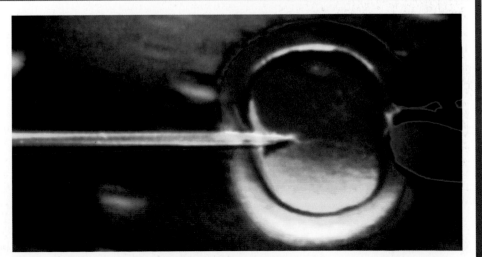

⬆ *Male genetic material is added to the egg cell through a very narrow hollow needle.*

Each human body starts as a tiny speck, the fertilized egg. Nine months later it is six billion times bigger – a newborn baby, which can cry loudly when it is very tired or hungry! The time of development in the mother's womb is known as pregnancy.

➡ As the speck-like fertilized egg develops into a baby, most of the body parts form within the first two months. The mother's abdomen begins to bulge from about 16 weeks after fertilization. She can feel the baby moving from about 18 weeks, as it twitches its arms, kicks its legs and bends its neck and back.

Which body parts develop first?

An unborn baby develops 'head-first', starting with the brain and head, then the main body, then the arms and legs. Life begins when the fertilized egg divides into two cells, then four, eight, and so on. After a few days there are hundreds of cells, and after a few weeks, millions. These cells build up the various body parts.

When does the heart start to beat?

The unborn baby's heart begins to beat after only four weeks, although it has not yet taken on its full shape. From the time of fertilization to eight weeks later, the developing baby is known as an embryo. The lungs, intestines and other parts are also taking shape around this time. In fact, by eight weeks all the main parts have formed, even the fingers and toes – yet the tiny body is only the size of a grape.

Can an unborn baby hear?

From before halfway through pregnancy, the unborn baby may be startled and move suddenly by a loud noise, indicating that it can hear. From eight weeks after fertilization until birth, the unborn baby is known as a foetus. It spends most of this time growing in size and developing smaller body parts such as eyelids, fingernails and toenails. In the womb it is dark, with nothing to see, yet the eyes are working, too, even though the lids are closed.

How does the unborn baby breathe?

It does not – it is surrounded and protected by bag-like membranes and fluids. However, it still needs oxygen to survive. This comes from the mother. The baby's blood flows along the twisted, rope-like umbilical cord to a plate-shaped part, the placenta, in the lining of the womb. Here the baby's blood passes very close to the mother's blood and oxygen can easily seep or diffuse into the baby's blood, which then flows back along the umbilical cord to its body. The baby is fed by nutrients in the same way.

Seeing the unborn baby

Ultrasound scans

In most regions of the world, a pregnant woman attends for regular check-ups at a medical centre or antenatal (before birth) clinic. The checks make sure that both she and the developing baby are healthy. One of the commonest tests is an ultrasound scan, which produces a picture of the baby in the womb. Tests on the mother's blood and urine, and checking her blood pressure, are also common. If there are problems, the

medical staff may give the mother substances to start the birth process early, called induction, or decide to deliver the baby by Caesarean section. Babies born earlier than usual, before the nine months of pregnancy are complete, are known as premature.

➡ An ultrasound scan uses a pen-like probe moved over the skin to show an image of the unborn baby on a screen, which helps doctors to determine that the baby is healthy and developing well.

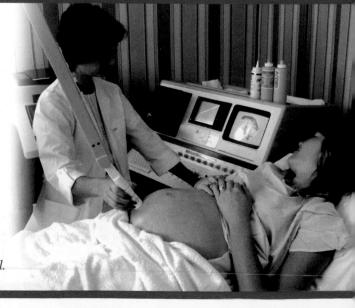

What happens at the start of birth?

As the time of birth approaches, powerful muscles in the wall of the womb begin to shorten or contract. This squeezes the baby through the opening or neck of the womb, called the cervix. The cervix was tightly closed during pregnancy but now widens, or dilates, to let the baby through. The contractions of the womb continue to push the baby along the birth canal, or vagina, until it emerges and is born.

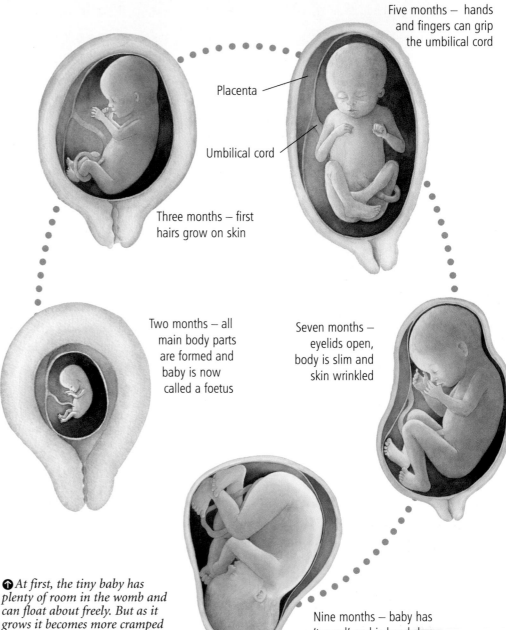

Five months — hands and fingers can grip the umbilical cord

Placenta

Umbilical cord

Three months — first hairs grow on skin

Two months — all main body parts are formed and baby is now called a foetus

Seven months — eyelids open, body is slim and skin wrinkled

Nine months — baby has 'turned' and is head-down, ready to be born

⬆ *At first, the tiny baby has plenty of room in the womb and can float about freely. But as it grows it becomes more cramped and has to bend its neck, back, arms and legs.*

⬆ *In order to keep fit whilst pregnant, and to prepare for birth, an expectant mother can undertake certain exercises and develop special breathing techniques.*

Problem **births**

• Most babies are born head-first, known as cephalic presentation. This is the safest way, since the baby's head is its widest part and gently makes the cervix open wide, so the rest of the body follows easily.

• Some babies are not in the right position in the womb to be born this way. For example the baby may be born positioned bottom-first, known as breech presentation.

• It may be possible for a doctor to turn the baby from outside, by pushing or massaging the mother's abdomen, so it can be born head-first.

• In some cases the baby gets stuck. One option is to use a spoon-like device called forceps which fit around the baby's head and help to ease it out of the womb.

• Another option is to make an incision (cut) in the mother's abdomen and womb wall, remove the baby through this, and stitch or fasten the incision so it heals. This is known as a Caesarean birth.

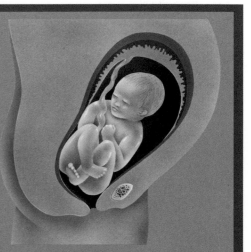

⬆ *In a breech birth, the baby's bottom may get stuck in the cervix.*

A newborn baby is about one-twentieth of the size of a fully-grown adult. But growth is about far more than getting bigger. Body shape and proportions change, muscles become stronger and movements more skilled. From the moment of birth, the baby learns an incredible amount almost every day.

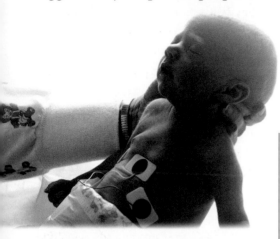

⬆ *A newborn baby is given an extensive medical check-up, in this case with sensor pads to monitor heartbeat rate. The baby's head is so large and heavy compared to its neck and body muscles, it needs to be carefully supported to prevent damage.*

What does a newborn baby do?

A new baby seems to do little except cry, feed on its mother's milk and sleep. At first it probably sleeps for about 20 hours in every 24. But the baby can carry out various automatic actions, or reflexes. It grips something that touches its hand and turns its head towards anything that touches its cheek. If startled by a loud noise, it throws out its arms and cries. And when its bladder and bowels are full, it empties them straight away!

When does walking start?

On average a baby can walk at around one year of age. Most babies learn to do more complicated actions, such as walking and talking, in the same order. But the times may differ widely, and being early to talk or late to walk is rarely a problem. Most babies can sit up by themselves at five to six months, stand whilst supported at seven to eight months, crawl at eight to nine months, and walk at about one year old. These movements are called motor skills.

⬆ *Babies can smile as young as a few weeks old, and can laugh within the first year. On average, babies start to talk from about ten months old.*

When does talking begin?

Like motor (movement) skills, the process of learning to talk happens at widely varying ages in different babies. Some can say several simple words like 'dada', 'mama' and 'cat' by the age of ten months, while others may not begin to form words until 13 to 14 months. Putting words together, like 'teddy bear' starts at about 14 to 15 months. By 18 months old the average toddler knows 20 or more words.

⬅ *Some babies crawl at six months – but some never do. They may use other methods such as rolling over or shuffling along on their bottoms to move about, before they begin to walk.*

Years of change

Puberty
The age at which puberty begins varies, from eight to nine years old up to 14 to 15 years. This depends on features such as body size and availability of healthy food, while illness can delay or slow the process. In general, the changes take two to three years in girls and three to four years in boys. The changes occur, on average, two years earlier in girls than in boys.

⬆ *Girls go through both a physical and mental change during puberty.*

Changes at puberty

• During childhood, girls and boys are similar in height. During puberty, both sexes rapidly become taller. But, on average, boys grow more, and so usually end up taller adults than girls.

• Girls develop a more rounded body outline, especially on the shoulders and hips, while boys become more angular, with broader shoulders.

• The reproductive or menstrual cycle begins in girls, while the reproductive organs in the male body begin to make sperm cells.

When does the body grow fastest?

After birth, the fastest time of growth is during the first year, when body weight increases about three times. Then growth gradually slows until the age of about 9 to 12 years, when it speeds up again. This time of fast growth through the early teenage years is known as puberty. It includes rapid development of the reproductive or sexual parts, as these begin to work.

⬇ *Teenagers may interact with one another to develop social skills, which can become the basis for future relationships in life.*

⬆ *Young children often think little about risks and dangers, such as falling over during play – which could cause a serious injury and even life-long harm. Adults need to point out the hazards and the need for safety precautions such as protective clothing and equipment.*

When is the body fully-grown?

Most people reach their full height by about 20 years of age. The muscles reach their full development at about 25 years. However, some physical activities involve co-ordination, training, practise and mental preparation as well as simple muscle power. Some sports people do not reach their peak until 30-plus years of age. Body weight is more variable – certain people alter their body weight, up and down, throughout life.

⬇ *The body grows not only physically, but also mentally – in the mind. This involves social skills such as making friends, respecting the opinions of others, understanding right and wrong and working out risks.*

Changes **in later life**

The changes of ageing are even more varied in their timing, than development when young. Some people begin to show signs of age from 40 years old, while others continue to look youthful at 60. In general, the changes in later life include:

- Hair becomes lighter, grey or perhaps white. Hair loss is also common, especially in men.

- Skin becomes less flexible and more wrinkled.

- Senses become less sharp, so that spectacles may be needed for eyesight, and a hearing aid to clarify sounds.

- Muscles begin to lose power from about 35 to 40 years old.

- Reactions become slower -- about half the speed at 65 years of age compared to their speed at the age of 20.

- The heart and lungs gradually lose efficiency, with less stamina or 'staying power' for lengthy exercise.

- A century ago, the average lifespan for a person in a developed country was 50 years. Today, it has increased to 72 to 75 for men, and 76 to 79 for women.

⬆ *Some people enjoy good health at 80 years old or more.*

Why not test your knowledge on the human body! Try answering these questions to find out how much you know about bones, joints, cells, organs, body systems, how human beings are created and much more. Questions are grouped into the subject areas covered within the pages of this book. See how much you remember and discover how much more you can learn.

Lungs and Breathing

15 Which gas does your body take in when you breathe?
16 Does incoming air pass through your lungs or your windpipe first?
17 What does exhalation mean?

Find Out About the Body

1 Your body is made up of 50 per cent, 70 per cent or 90 per cent of water?
2 Where is your skin thickest?
3 The science of the body and its parts is called what?

Skin, Hair and Nails

4 Which two parts of your body do you brush every day?
5 What do you have five million of growing on your body?
6 You would find a cuticle at the base of which parts of the body?

7 A tendon connects a muscle to what type of body part?

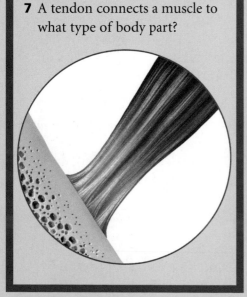

8 Heart valves ensure that blood pumping to and from the heart does what?

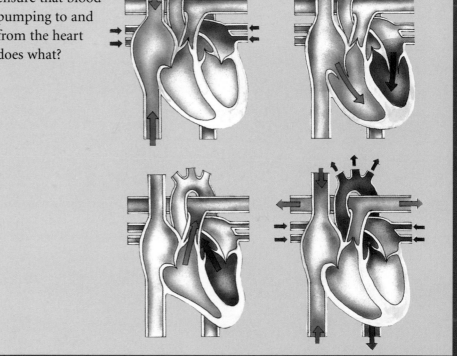

Bones and Joints

9 How many bones make up the skeleton?
10 How many pairs of ribs do you have?
11 Which is the longest bone in your body?

Muscles and Moving

12 What pulls your bones and lets you move?
13 Where are your strongest muscles?
14 Which muscle is in the back of the leg, below the knee?

Eating and Digestion

18 What gives your body energy?
19 Is your stomach above or below your intestines?
20 Which is longer: your small or large intestine?

Heart and Blood

21 What causes a bruise to turn blue?
22 What carries blood away from the heart?
23 Which type of blood cells carry oxygen?

24 Which part of the throat tightens across the airway and vibrates in order to produce sound?

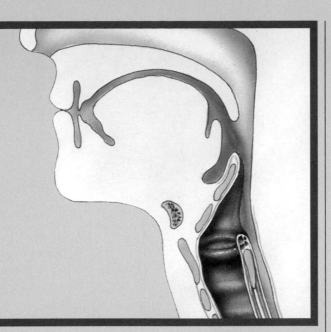

Start of a New Body

37 What is the name for three babies born at the same time?
38 What part of the mother does a baby grow in?
39 If a disease is hereditary, how does someone catch it?

The Body Before Birth

40 What is the name of the tube that supplies nourishment to a baby before it is born?
41 How many months are there between conception and birth?
42 What do we call a baby that is born before it is fully developed?

Body Wastes and Defences

25 What forms over a cut when it is healing?
26 What should you do before you eat or drink?
27 If you take medicine orally, how do you take it?

Senses

28 What are the five senses?
29 What part of your body do you see with?
30 Why is blinking good for your eyes?

Nerves and Brain

31 Do you get goose pimples when you are hot or cold?
32 Which part of your body helps you keep your balance?
33 What does the spine protect?

Working Brain

34 The optic nerve leads to the brain from where?
35 What is amnesia?
36 What do we call an automatic response by a muscle, which does not involve thinking?

The Growing Body

43 What is a newborn baby's main food?
44 Do you grow more when you are awake or when you are asleep?
45 What happens to a boy's voice when it breaks?

Answers

1 70 per cent
2 The soles of your feet
3 Anatomy
4 Your hair and teeth
5 Hairs
6 Fingernails and toenails
7 Bones
8 Make it flow one way
9 206
10 12
11 Thigh bone
12 Muscles

13 In your jaw
14 The calf
15 Oxygen
16 Windpipe
17 Breathing-out
18 Food
19 Above
20 Small intestine
21 Blood from broken veins
22 Arteries
23 Red blood cells
24 Vocal cords

25 A scab
26 Wash your hands
27 By mouth
28 Sight, hearing, touch, smell and taste
29 Your eyes
30 It keeps them clean
31 Cold
32 Your ears
33 Spinal chord
34 The eyes
35 Loss of memory
36 A reflex

37 Triplets
38 Womb
39 It is inherited from both parents
40 Umbilical chord
41 Nine
42 Premature
43 Milk
44 Asleep
45 It sounds deeper

Page numbers in **bold** refer to main subjects, page numbers in *italics* refer to illustrations.

The publishers would like to thank the following artists who have contributed to this book:
June Allan, Syd Brak, Mark Davis, Mike Foster, Janos Marffy, Martin Sanders, Mike Saunders, Guy Smith, Rudi Vizi

The publishers wish to thank the following sources for the photographs used in this book:
Michal Heron/CORBIS p22 (b/r) ; JEAN-CHRISTOPHE VERHAEGEN-PIG/AFP/GETTY IMAGES p27 (b/r);
Lester Lefkowitz/CORBIS p31 (b/r); EDELMANN/SCIENCE PHOTO LIBRARY p32 (t/c); Norbert Schaefer/CORBIS p33 (c/l)

All other photographs are from:
Corel, digitalSTOCK, PhotoDisc, STOCKBYTE